Table of Contents

I0493958

Unit 4C, concepts of law, is *synoptic*. This means it connects to your other areas of study, not just the substantive law, but the institutions and procedures. You will be expected to show your understanding of these by relating them to the various concepts of law. In this booklet, we cover 'Law and Morals'. You should also be able to relate this concept to more contemporary issues and you will find plenty of examples here.

The theory of law is called *jurisprudence*, and is a compulsory part of most law degrees. Many academics, philosophers and judges have written about the theory of law, and there is much disagreement between them.

Examination tip

You are not expected to 'take sides' when discussing the various arguments. You may wish to state your own opinion but if so, be sure to back this up with reference to the theorists and to relevant cases. The main thing when it comes to the examination is to have a clear focus and keep your answer centred on the specific question asked, i.e., keep your answer and examples relevant and, where possible, use one or two of the theorists to support what you say.

There is no strict definition of what amounts to 'morality'. A common definition is 'a set of rules which govern a group's behaviour'. This sounds a bit like law too, and legal and moral rules can overlap. However, some laws do not have a moral element and many moral rules are not enshrined in law.

Some see law and morals as separate, and we will look at some of the different views later, but first an example of a moral rule that is not a legal one.

Example

A common example used is that of a person walking past someone who is drowning and taking no action. Asked whether it is a crime not to try to save them, many students answer 'yes', but in the UK the answer is 'no'. There is usually no criminal liability for a failure to act, an omission. You might say, 'Well, you *should* try to save them.' This is a **moral** issue. You may have a **moral** duty to act but you have no **legal** duty to do so. As our law stands, it is left to the individual. This is what law and morals is all about; the question of how far the law *is*, and *should be*, imposing rules and how far any action should be left to individual choice.

Many cases involve several different concepts so you will see cases repeated in the other 'Law Explained' booklets on concepts. Other than cases from the substantive law e.g., crime, tort or contract, there are many contemporary issues which will involve these concepts of law, such as whether it is right to force-feed an anorexic, whether separating Siamese twins knowing one will die is morally justified, whether gays should have equal marriage rights to heterosexuals and many others.

Examination tip

It is useful to learn and fully understand cases that can be used across the Unit well, because you can use the same one in different questions - as long as you change the focus. For the higher mark bands, especially in 'Law and Morals' and 'Law and Justice' you should also refer to the theorists on the area to develop your points. You can also develop your point by arguing for or against the decision.

Example

Taking the case of **Brown**, we can look at how that case can be used to discuss each of the five concepts in Unit 4C AQA Law. This is a very brief outline, as you have not covered all these concepts.

However, it should give you an idea of how you can use a case and then adapt and develop it to different situations – a bit like judges do with law.

	Whether sexual violence in private should be regulated by law rather than purely a matter of morality	**Devlin** would say 'yes' because immoral acts undermine the fabric of society, even when done in private **Hart** would say 'no' because law and morals should be kept separate **Mill** might say 'yes' because he believed in non-interference in individual rights, but could say 'no' because he added 'unless doing so could harm others'
	Whether justice is achieved by imposing legal sanctions against certain behaviour even if it occurs in private	The above could be used again but also a **Utilitarian** would want to see the greatest benefit for the greatest number so could argue that this is achieved by banning the behaviour of the minority to protect society as a whole
	Earlier cases conflicted on whether consent was a defence to serious injuries, the majority indicated the ratio was that it was not	Where a *ratio* is unclear, later judges can select the most appropriate or can distinguish the case on the facts. **Professor Goodhard** said, "*It is by his choice of material facts that the judge creates law*" Arguably with such a serious crime Parliament rather than unelected judges should create the law
	It was unclear whether the decision was based on the amount of harm or whether the harm was intentional	*Mens rea* is an important element of criminal law and where harm is committed with intent it should be penalised The acts had been consented to, so it is wrong that the law penalised the behaviour. Even though there was MR the consent defence should have succeeded
	The interests of the public to be protected from violence had to be balanced against the interests of the individuals to act as they pleased in private	**Devlin** would say that society had to be protected from evil, as did some of the judges in **Brown**. **Lord Lowry** said sadomasochism was "*not conducive to the welfare of society*", and so a **Utilitarian** might agree with the decision. **Pound** believed that public and private interests should not be balanced against each other as the public interest will always prevail, as seen here

The tasks are intended to reinforce your learning so do these as you go along. The answers are at the end of the booklet. Some tasks will just ask you to jot down a few thoughts for use in an essay, so there are no answers to these, but keep your notes for revision and exam practice. I have included occasional quotes so use these too; they show that you know what judges have to say about the law.

A brief reminder: Criminal cases are usually in the form *R v the defendant*. It is acceptable to use just the name so if the case is **R v Miller** I have called it **Miller**. If another form is used, e.g., **DPP v Miller** I have used the full title, as you may want to look up the case for further information. Civil cases are between the *claimant* and the *defendant*, although you will see the word '*plaintiff*' in cases before 1999.

There is a list of some common abbreviations in the appendix at the end of the booklet.

Task 1

Consider whether the following are/should be illegal or immoral. If possible, ask a friend to do this too. See if you agree.

Murder

Smoking in public

Cheating in examinations

Speeding

Swearing in public

Shoplifting

Adultery

Lying

Parking on a double yellow line

'… there remains an area of private morality and immorality that is not the law's business'

The Wolfenden Report, 1957

There is a significant overlap between morality and law but much disagreement over how far they do, and should, overlap – I doubt you and your friend agreed on everything in the above task. Crimes such as murder, theft and rape are generally held to be immoral as well as illegal. Not all crimes are seen as immoral, for example, traffic offences. However, even parking on a yellow line is arguably immoral if you are blocking an emergency exit. Adultery, swearing and cheating are not illegal but may be viewed as immoral. Lying may be immoral, and is sometimes illegal, e.g., lying in court or in certain documents. Shoplifting is theft, but some would argue it isn't morally wrong to take a bone from a butcher's shop to feed a starving dog. The ban on smoking which came into force in 2007 under the **Health Act 2006** is an example of the overlap. Many argue that the law should not interfere; that it is a matter of individual choice. Others argue that smoking can harm others, so should be illegal. Similar debates arose over the banning of foxhunting, which was a moral issue but is now illegal too.

Here is a summary of the main differences between moral rules and legal rules.

- Develop gradually over time and don't change overnight
- *Should* be obeyed
- Are enforced by the disapproval of friends, family and society
- Are voluntary and apply to those who willingly accept them and agree to be bound by them

- Can change quickly by Acts of Parliament or court cases
- *Must* be obeyed
- Are enforced by legal sanctions through the courts
- Are not voluntary and apply to everyone

The theories of justice (dealt with in detail in the 'Law and Justice – the law explained' booklet) are useful when looking at the connection between law and morals. Here is a very brief description of the two main ones.

Natural law – morality and law are interlinked

The Natural Law theory regards law as coming from a higher source such as God or nature. Under this theory, all laws are based on moral rules and if they not then they are not true laws. Natural Law theorists would argue that the law must follow some 'higher natural law', and if it did not then it

5

would not be a real law and should not normally be obeyed. An example of a person taking the natural law view is Lord Devlin, discussed below.

Positivists have tried to find a more scientific way of describing law, without reference to morality. For positivists, law *may* be based on ideas of morality, but it is not *necessary* that it should be. The validity of law is not affected by whether it is morally acceptable. Most positivist theories attempt to explain what law *is* rather than what it *ought* to be. An example of a person taking the positivist view is Professor Hart, discussed below. Another is the philosopher John Stuart Mill. These views are described and compared under the section 'The relationship between law and morals'.

Diversity of moral views

Durkheim argued that in a plural society with diverse views there is no 'shared morality'. There is no single moral standard to apply. As with foxhunting and smoking, what some people see as immoral, others don't. What is regarded as immoral in one society, or in one time, may not be so in another. Adultery and abortion are other examples. These are legal but some believe them to be immoral, and in some countries, they are crimes. Even giving advice on contraception in order to avoid an unwanted pregnancy has been the subject of legal challenge. In **Gillick v West Norfolk and Wisbech AHA 1986**, a mother challenged her daughter's doctor for prescribing contraceptives. She lost at first instance, won in the CA and lost again in the HL by a majority of 3-2. No shared morality here either. The case became famous and led to children having greater rights to make their own decisions on such matters as medical treatment, as long as they are what is now called 'Gillick competent'.

In **Axon v Secretary of State for Health 2006**, a mother argued that the Gillick principle conflicted with **Article 8** of the **European Convention on Human Rights (ECHR)**, the right to family life. She said that parents had a right to be informed about children seeking advice or treatment on sexual issues. The CA held that parental rights reduce as the child gets older and more knowledgeable. Confirming the principle of 'Gillick competence', the CA held that the right to be informed ceases to exist once the child is competent to make his or her own decisions. This shows that there may be a duty for the law to be involved in moral issues to protect young children, but that as the child gets older the law should leave the issues to the individual concerned.

The law needs to keep up with changes in technology as well as social views. Advances in medical technology led to the setting up of the **Warnock Committee**. This looked at several issues involving in-vitro fertilisation (IVF), including the use of embryos in medical research. It reported in 1984 and many of its findings were included in the **Human Fertilisation and Embryology Act 1990**. There is still much debate on the subject and opinion is divided, e.g., on IVF technology and the creation of 'designer babies', discussed below.

Both law and morals involve rules. The courts enforce the law, but not social rules. However, if the morality is shared then most people will obey the rules. The question is should moral issues be a matter for society alone, or should the law promote and/or enforce morality? The problem with making social rules into legal ones is the conflict of opinion about most moral issues. If morality is not shared then *whose* values should the law reflect when promoting or enforcing morals? The difficulties were recognised at the time of the Committee report. Mary Warnock, the academic who chaired the committee, made this point:

"I do not believe there is a neat way of marking off moral issues from all others; some people, at some time, may regard things as matters of moral right and moral wrong, which at another time or in another place are thought to be matters of taste, or of no importance at all."

Social rules can be enforced by society's disapproval of any breach of the rules. Jumping the queue at the supermarket checkout to get your shopping home earlier isn't illegal but few of us do it.

Legal rules are enforced by the police and the courts. Jumping the traffic lights to get your shopping home earlier *is* illegal.

Imagine you are with a group of people stranded on a desert island. You need to make some rules to govern behaviour. Make a list of six rules you think are important. Now go on to decide if they should have the force of law. How will they be enforced?

Examination tip

Read the question carefully. You may be asked how far the law *promotes* moral values, if so discuss laws which actively seek to make society behave in a certain way. Examples would be laws banning smoking and fox hunting. These laws aim to promote morality by providing new rules. If asked how far the law *enforces* moral values then emphasise laws which *reflect* society's views. A case example is **R v R 1991**, where the HL abolished the rule that a man could not be guilty of raping his wife. Previously, this was not rape as the woman was deemed to have consented to sex by virtue of marriage. However, society no longer regarded women as the property of their husbands, and in their judgment the Law Lords reflected this view.

In 2004, a Russian newspaper carried a report that Moscow city authorities were considering a ban on kissing and embracing on the underground. The *Stolichnaya Vechernaya* said the ban, aimed at raising public morality, could even extend to a husband embracing his wife. This may be a Russian case but it is a clear example of a government promoting moral values via the law.

The relationship between law and morals

The relationship between law and morality is complex and questions arise as to whether one is shaped by the other. If so, which shapes which – and which *should* shape which? Does the law decide what is 'moral' or does society's view of morality shape the law?

One major report about the law, and how far it should reflect morality, is the **Wolfenden Committee Report 1957** on homosexuality and prostitution. This said the purposes of the criminal law are:

"... to preserve public order and decency, to protect the citizen from what is offensive and injurious and to provide sufficient safeguards against exploitation and corruption of others especially the vulnerable ... The law should not intervene in the private lives of citizens or seek to enforce any particular pattern of behaviour further than necessary to carry out the above purposes."*

The opening quote came from this report. The committee recommended that prostitution and homosexual acts between consenting adult males in private should no longer be criminal offences. However, activities associated with prostitution, which could cause offence to others (such as soliciting in the street), were still to be regulated by the law.

The **Wolfenden Report** became the subject of a major legal debate between **Lord Devlin**, a judge who took the view that law and morality are inextricably linked, and **Professor Hart**, an academic who argued that there is no widely shared morality.

View 1 – law and morality are separate

Hart argued that using the law to enforce morality was unnecessary, undesirable and morally unacceptable.

Unnecessary because society would not otherwise disintegrate

Undesirable because it would freeze morality at that time

Unacceptable because it would restrict the freedom of the individual

Hart was heavily influenced by John Stuart Mill, and he approved of the commission's approach to liberalising the laws.

Example

A case where the law accorded with Hart's view and refused to enforce morality was **R (on the application of Green) v City of Westminster Magistrates' Court 2007**. A member of Christian Voice argued that the play 'Jerry Springer: the Opera' was a blasphemous libel and so an offence at common law. The court held that for this offence there not only had to be an attack on Christianity in some way but it also had to 'endanger society' by 'depraving public morality' or causing civil strife. The court found that, as regards the second element, the play had been showing in London for two years without any such effect on society. Another example is **Gillick** where the decision of the court favoured the rights of the individual child.

View 2 – law and morality are linked

Lord **Devlin** was vehemently against Hart's viewpoint. He argued that immoral acts, even in private, could weaken the fabric of society and that society should punish an act thought grossly offensive and immoral by the standards of the 'right-minded person'. This begs the questions – how do we identify the content of this morality and who are these right-minded people?

Examples

Two older cases illustrate support for Lord Devlin's view. In **Shaw v DPP 1961,** arguments for upholding a conviction for 'conspiring to corrupt public morals' (by publishing a directory of prostitutes) rested on the need to *"conserve the moral welfare of the state"*. In **Knuller v DPP 1973 HL,** the court convicted the Ds for publishing advertisements for homosexuals. Although the **Sexual Offences Act 1967** had made homosexuality legal following the Wolfenden Report, Lord Reid said,

"… if people choose to corrupt themselves in this way that is their affair and the law will not interfere. But no licence is given to others to encourage this practice."

These cases suggest that the law will interfere where others are encouraged to immorality, and not where it is a private matter. The link between law and morality is there, but perhaps not to the extent that Devlin would like to see. Similarly, with prostitution, this is legal, but other people who make money from the practice, such as brothel keepers and pimps, are committing an offence. Even though the Wolfenden Committee recommended that homosexuality and prostitution be legalised, they also recognised that one of the functions of the law is to provide safeguards against the exploitation and corruption of others, and this view is reflected in the laws which followed.

The philosopher's view

The philosopher **John Stuart Mill (1806 – 1873)**, would have agreed with the Committee. His view was that the law should leave people to make their own choices, so long as they do not harm others. Mill attempted to develop the utilitarian view (that law should attempt to produce the maximum benefit for the maximum number) to take into account individual rights. He said that the law should only prohibit actions that harm others, not those which are merely offensive. Law and morals should be separate because if a law is based on moral values it is not treating people equally (as one person's values are being upheld and another's not). Many lawyers and judges have been influenced by this view.

The case of **R (on the application of Green) v City of Westminster Magistrates' Court 2007**, above, accords with Mill's view, as freedom of expression was upheld on the basis that the public were not harmed. Similarly, in **Gillick** the freedom of the individual child prevailed over the mother's wishes to be informed. In neither case was the moral view reflected by the law.

Against Mill's view, it can be argued that very few actions have no effect on others. Look back to the smoking argument for an example of this point.

In **Brown 1994**, the HL held that, where the Ds had committed homosexual sadomasochistic acts, resulting in injuries, public policy demanded that these acts be treated as unlawful even though they occurred in private and the participants had consented. There was not only disagreement in the decision (a 3-2 majority), but in the reasoning behind it showing a diversity of views among the Law Lords.

Lord Templeman said, "Society is entitled and bound to protect itself against a cult of violence. Pleasure derived from the infliction of pain is an evil thing."

Lord Lowry said such activities were not *"conducive to the welfare of society"*. Both these statements accord with Devlin's view and are examples of the law reflecting morality. However, the two dissenting judges were more in line with Hart, that law and morality were not inextricably linked. Lord Mustill took the view that although the acts were immoral that did not make them unlawful and the conviction should be quashed. Lord Slynn said it was not for the courts to protect people from themselves.

N.B.: The European Court of Human Rights upheld the majority view in **Brown**.

The fact that the decision was influenced by the judges' views of what was morally acceptable can be seen by comparing it to **Wilson 1996,** where D was acquitted after branding his initials on his wife's buttocks.

Do you think Mill would have approved of the ban on smoking or not?

What do you think Mill's view would have been had he been a judge in **Brown**?

It can be argued that judges are not the right people to decide issues of morality. If these issues are not to be left to individual choice, should it be for Parliament alone to lay down the law? In **Gibson 1991**, an artist exhibited earrings made from freeze-dried foetuses. He was convicted of the common law offence of outraging public decency. Society may be 'outraged' but has it been harmed? Mill would probably argue that the law should not interfere.

Here are a few examples of how law and morals relate to crime, contract, tort and contemporary issues.

Read the following examples carefully, but use your own too. You will produce a better essay if you use cases you know well to support any discussion about law and morals. Also, note that your argument is not about right and wrong, but whether the matter should be classed as a legal issue or a matter of personal choice. You may have strong views about the morality of hunting for example, but when discussing this you need to relate your argument to how far the law should restrict this activity, using the theorists in support.

Criminal law has plenty of examples because many crimes have a moral element, especially offences against the person.

Brown is an obvious example of enforcing morality. Devlin would agree with the decision in **Brown**, and argue that the law needed to step in to protect society against evil. Hart and Mill would say it is not the law's place to enforce moral values. **Wilson** can be used in comparison – did the judges decide differently on moral grounds? You can use cases on murder and manslaughter to support a discussion about the right to life – and death. Although killing is usually regarded as both immoral and illegal, there are situations where there may be a moral case for killing, as in euthanasia and assisted suicide discussed below. In **Bland** and **Re A**, doctors had to make a moral decision to end a life, but needed the court to confirm there would be no legal repercussions. Failing to save a life may be immoral but not usually illegal, but in cases such as **Stone & Dobinson** and **Gibbins & Proctor** there was a duty to act and so criminal liability arose.

The rules on the defences of insanity and automatism recognise that the law should not punish someone who does not know they are doing wrong. On the other hand, the limitations on the intoxication defence reflect society's view that drinking should not excuse criminal activity. The defence of consent has been discussed above. It was refused in **Brown** but allowed in **Wilson** on what seemed to be moral rather than legal grounds. Consent is not accepted as a defence to murder but there have been challenges to this in cases where people are too severely disabled to take their own lives and wish a doctor or family member to assist, as in **Pretty**. It is a difficult moral question, not only because of the right to die or the right to life debate, but also because there is a fine line between assisted suicide and murder. In 2012, the High Court refused an application by a severely disabled man challenging the laws governing the right to die, saying it was for Parliament to decide. Parliament is, however, reluctant to address the issue as public opinion is so divided. The man, Mr Lamb, is to take his case to the Court of Appeal in 2013.

As for property offences, theft can be related to the argument that stealing from the rich and giving to the poor is not immoral, although it is certainly illegal. Similarly, taking food to feed a child, or a bone to feed a starving dog, may not be seen as immoral to some people, but theft is illegal whatever the motive. In many cases of criminal damage caused during protest campaigns, the protesters have tried to use the defence that they have a moral right to protect property from, e.g., nuclear power or GM crops. However, this defence has so far failed. In **DPP v Blake 1993**, a vicar wrote biblical quotations on a wall outside Parliament and claimed that he had God's consent to cause criminal damage. He also failed. In these cases, moral arguments have been subjugated to legal rules.

Although contract is an area with fewer moral issues, there are still examples to be found. Contract is based on the exchange of promises and the law will impose sanctions on those who break their promises, as in **Ruxley Electronics**, where D was awarded damages for breach of a contract term regarding the depth of the swimming pool. Generally, though, the courts are reluctant to interfere in the making of contracts based on 'freedom of contract'. This is in accord with Mill's argument that the law should not interfere unless harm will result. This can include economic harm so you could discuss the way both Parliament and the courts *will* interfere to protect the weaker party in consumer contracts, e.g., by imposing terms (**SGA/SOGSA/The Moorcock**) and by limiting the ability of a business to exclude liability (**UCTA**) or impose unfair terms (**UTCCR**). The courts will also interfere where an agreement is the result of misrepresentation, duress or fraud.

Donoghue shows the courts are prepared to develop the law to protect the consumer. A moral link can be seen in the biblical idea of 'love thy neighbour' which Lord Atkin developed to 'do not harm your neighbour' when establishing whether someone owed another a duty of care. In **White,** the police were unable to succeed in a claim for psychiatric harm following a football stadium disaster. This was partly because it would be immoral to allow the police to get compensation but not the victims' families whose claims had already failed. In **Greatorex**, the court thought it undesirable to allow members of a family to sue each other. In **BRB v Herrrington**, the HL held BR owed a 'common duty of humanity' to a child trespasser and later, Parliament reflected and enforced this morality by passing the **Occupiers' Liability Act 1984** to increase the level of care expected by an occupier of premises.

Task 4

The following all came from the judgements in **Brown**. Which theorist do you think would agree with which comment?

Lord Lowry said such activities were not *"conducive to the welfare of society"*.

Lord Mustill took the view that although the acts were immoral that did not make them unlawful, and the conviction should be quashed.

Lord Slynn said it was not for the courts to protect people from themselves.

Essay pointer

Should the law reflect and enforce morality? This depends on your view of law and the purposes it serves in society. Whether judges (rather than Parliament) should develop the law to enforce morality is another question. It is argued that judges are appointed rather than elected and not accountable to the people, so should not attempt to impose their views on others. On the other hand, it can be argued that they are independent, more objective and don't have to give way to popular fashion or keep the electorate happy. Development of the law can involve judges in questions of morality. This is arguably the role of Parliament where the issues can be fully debated. In **Quintavalle**, below, the pressure group CORE said the decision was *"certainly a defeat for parliamentary democracy."*

Contemporary examples of the overlap between law and morals

'Designer' babies

There is much debate about whether or not people should be able to choose the genetic make-up of their babies. Many argue that this should not be done for social reasons, e.g., to balance the number of boys and girls in a family. However, where there are medical reasons, it is perhaps more acceptable. This moral question also raises legal issues. It was the subject of **Quintavalle v Human Fertilisation and Embryology Authority 2005**. A couple had been granted the right by the Authority to use 'tissue typing' to select an embryo that would be a match for their son, who was seriously ill and needed a transplant. This would mean an embryo that was not a match would be discarded. The pressure group CORE (Comment on Reprographic Ethics) challenged the Authority's right to do so under the **Human Fertilisation and Embryology Act 1990**. They argued that it could lead to people being able to have embryos tested (and discarded) for other characteristics, such as sex or hair colour – hence the term 'designer' babies. The HL, whilst recognising the case raised *"profound ethical questions"*, ruled that the **Act** could be interpreted as allowing selection. In August 2005, the government issued a consultation paper to assess public opinion on these issues. This resulted in the **Human Fertilisation and Embryology Act 2008** which was brought into effect over 2009/2010 and amends the **1990 Act**. Tissue typing can be licensed under the later **Act** where a sibling suffers from a serious medical condition, putting the decision in **Quintavalle** into statutory form. Also, although sex selection on social grounds is prohibited, the Act allows it if serious harm could otherwise occur, e.g., through a gender-related hereditary disease. This clarifies the earlier law and brings it up to date with medical advances – at least for the moment. This is an example of a moral issue being put into an Act of Parliament, which is arguably better than relying on interpretation by the courts on such a controversial subject.

In 2003, a couple had to go to America to complete treatment after being refused it in the UK. The first time that the full treatment was done in Britain was in 2010 after the **2008 Act** came into force. Megan Matthews was born with a rare blood disorder and needed transfusions every few weeks. She received tissue donated by her brother who had been created for this purpose. The doctors recognised that there were ethical concerns about creating children with specific genetic material, but said that these were outweighed by the benefits. In addition, the parents had wanted another child anyway, but if conceived naturally, there was a strong possibility that the child would have the same disease.

Euthanasia and assisted suicide

Since the case of Diane Pretty in 2002 there have been many cases challenging the law on assisted suicide. She had tried to get immunity from prosecution for her husband if he helped her to die but her arguments failed to persuade the HL. In **R (Purdy) v DPP 2009**, Mrs Purdy argued that the law on assisted suicide as it stands is unclear and unfair. The CA relied on **Pretty** and noted that as that was a decision of the HL it must be followed as a binding precedent. However, on appeal the Law Lords were unanimous in deciding that the DPP should issue clearer guidance on the criteria used when deciding whether to prosecute in cases of assisted suicide. The decision reflects the changing opinion of society in general on suicide, and on whether those who help someone to commit suicide should be prosecuted. However, although guidelines were published in 2010, the DPP said at the time *"The policy does not change the law on assisted suicide. It does not open the door for euthanasia"* and that each case has to be considered on its own facts and merits. Not much has really changed, although there have so far not been any prosecutions in respect of the 40 or so cases reported to the DPP since the guidelines were issued.

Between these two cases, there was a slightly more unusual one. In 2006, Mr Burke took a case to the ECHR not arguing the right to die, but the right to life. He was seriously ill and feared treatment could be withdrawn against his wishes. The court held that it was for doctors to decide in the particular circumstances of the individual case.

In **Nicklinson & Another 2013**, the law was challenged again. Mr Nicklinson died before the appeal but Mr Lamb and a man known as Martin continued the case. Martin's wife did not want to assist in his suicide so he would need a doctor's help. The guidelines issued in 2010 do not extend outside the family. The CA rejected the challenge and said any change to the law should be left to Parliament. However, they said the guidelines lacked sufficient clarity as to what the position would be if the person who assisted in the suicide were not closely connected to the victim.

These are difficult issues because there is a fine line between assisted suicide, euthanasia and murder. This was seen in the **Inglis** and **Gilderdale** cases, where the mothers had ended their severely disabled child's life. The first was murder because her son was unable to convey his wishes; the second was assisted suicide because her daughter had made her views clear and wanted to die.

In their 2004 report 'Partial Defences to Murder' the Law Commission said

> *"... the Government should undertake a public consultation on whether, and if so to what extent, the law should recognise either an offence of "mercy" killing or a partial defence of "mercy" killing".*

The emotive nature of the issue and the heated public debates mean it is unlikely that euthanasia will be made legal in England any time soon. It is legal in Belgium, which became the first country to allow euthanasia for children when a bill was passed by their Parliament in February 2014. Although no age limits are set, the bill says that the child must have 'a capacity of discernment and be conscious at the moment of the request'. This is similar to the law in England on other kinds of treatment, which requires children to be 'Gillick' competent before being able to make decisions on medical care.

There was much heated debate prior to the passing of the Belgian law, with church leaders and other groups arguing that the law is immoral. It only applies where a child is terminally ill, and has made repeated requests to die. The child must also face 'unbearable physical suffering' before euthanasia is considered as an option. Parents, doctors and psychiatrists would have to agree before a decision is made.

Even if not made legal here, if the government took up the Law Commission's other option and made euthanasia a partial defence along with diminished responsibility and loss of control, this would allow for discretion in sentencing and perhaps make juries more willing to convict. If killing is immoral then it is also immoral that someone should be acquitted because the jury are reluctant to see him or her get a life sentence.

Religious clothing and symbols

A further issue in relation to whether the law should be involved in what is essentially a moral issue arose in the case **R (Begum) v Denbigh High School 2006**, where a Muslim pupil took her school to court for refusing to allow her to wear a full length jilbab. She lost at first instance but the CA allowed her appeal. The case then went to the HL which ruled that the school had not acted unlawfully. The school had consulted with Muslim groups and parents on the subject of uniform and their policy was to allow pupils to wear a 'shalwar kameez' (a long top and trousers) but not the full jilbab.

In **Azmi v Kirklees Metropolitan Council 2006**, a support teacher, employed to help with teaching Year 6 students, insisted on wearing a full veil over her face. The head noticed that the children responded negatively and had trouble communicating with her because they could not see her face. She refused to comply with instructions not to wear the veil while teaching, and she was eventually suspended. The employment tribunal concluded that this was not discrimination on grounds of religion as any other teacher would have been treated in the same manner and, because the instruction was confined to the times she was actually teaching, it was a proportionate response.

In **R (on the application of X) v The Head Teacher of Y School 2007**, X was a 12-year-old Muslim girl at a girl's grammar school. At the start of her second year, she wore the niqab veil, which covered her entire face and head save for her eyes, when male teachers were teaching her. The head teacher told her that the wearing of the veil contravened school uniform policy, and if she continued to wear it she would be excluded. X argued that the refusal to allow her to wear the veil at school breached **Article 9 of the European Convention on Human Rights**, the right to manifest her religion or beliefs. Following **Begum** the court held that the school had not infringed her rights because there was the alternative of going to a school where she was allowed to wear one. In any case, the policy was justifiable and proportionate.

In **Eweida v British Airways 2010**, a Christian worker who was suspended from work for openly wearing a cross on a neck chain, in contravention of the company's dress code, failed in her attempt to prove she had been discriminated against. Previous company policy was to allow religious jewellery only if hidden from view and the CA rejected her claim that this discriminated against her on the grounds of religion. The CA held that such a policy was both proportionate and justified. In light of much debate on these issues, BA later agreed to allow staff to display a symbol of faith with their uniform. The employee has since returned to work, thereby gaining a moral, if not a legal, victory.

Gay marriage

Sometimes the law changes to reflect changing moral attitudes, as with the legalisation of prostitution following the Wolfenden Committee report. A more modern example is gay marriage.

Example

Gay marriage is an example of how laws have changed as society has changed its views, and shows the influence of morality upon the law. It is also an example of the length of time it takes for things to change. In 1895, the playwright Oscar Wilde was imprisoned for homosexual behaviour. The **Sexual Offences Act 1967** finally made homosexual acts in private legal (again following the Wolfenden Committee report). The **Civil Partnership Act 2004** allowed gay partnerships which allowed greater freedom for people of the same sex to enjoy many of the rights that married heterosexual couples have. Discrimination still existed however, and several cases went to the **European Court of Human Rights** arguing that same sex couples should enjoy the same rights as heterosexual ones. In response to changing public attitudes, in March 2014 gay marriage itself became legal when **s 1** of the **Marriage (Same Sex Couples) Act 2013** came into force.

These are difficult issues, and they highlight the problem with the law enforcing morality where opinions differ, where there is no 'shared morality'.

There are many other examples, such as smacking children, drinking in the street, withdrawing life-sustaining treatment etc. Look in the newspapers or watch the news and see if you can find something that interests you. One 2012 example from Russia concerned the punk group Pussy Riot. The group of female singers was convicted of blasphemy and imprisoned after singing protest songs in a cathedral. There was worldwide condemnation of the legal decision, including among most Russians who believed the court overreacted. Those who believe in individual freedoms, such as Mill, would agree; it may have been (arguably) immoral but no one was harmed and it should not have resulted in such severe legal sanctions, if any.

Task 5

In **Re E 2012**, a High Court judge ruled that a person suffering from anorexia could be force-fed against their wishes.

In **Re M 2011**, the High Court ruled that withdrawing artificial feeding from a patient in a coma was not in the patient's best interests despite the family wanting a declaration allowing the doctors to do this, as in **Bland**.

Do you think that the law should law decide whether someone could be fed against his or her wishes?

In **Bland,** withdrawing food was accepted; in **Re M,** it was not. Do you think that withdrawing artificial feeding from someone in a coma should be a matter for the law?

There is no 'right' answer here, you may argue for or against – or both.

Essay pointer

Some councils ban drinking on the street and other public places, some don't. It is arguable that this is a matter of morality rather than law, so should be left to individual choice (as Mill would argue). In addition, the law should be the same for everyone; it does not seem fair that what is legal in one area is illegal in another.

Choose two cases from your area of law, or other moral issue, plus two examples from the contemporary issues above. Then give one argument in favour of the law regulating such behaviour and one against it doing so, if possible mentioning one of the theorists. Arguing both for and against something, whichever side you would personally take, will help you produce a balanced argument when writing an essay.

Examination tip

Read the question carefully for specifics. Use cases and Acts to show the relationship between law and morals – or, if you prefer, to show there isn't one. There is no right answer and much debate regarding this relationship, so form your own opinion. Don't forget though; avoid voicing personal views too strongly, and ALWAYS support what you say with examples and academic discussion.

Self-test questions

Summarise the opposing views held by the Law Lords in **Brown***.*

What is the basic distinction between Hart and Devlin's views?

What was the outcome of **Quintavalle***?*

What is the **Wolfenden Report** *about?*

Make a list of three arguments that support your views in this area.

Revision

A general guide to revision

The first and foremost rule for revision is to start early. Too many students leave it until the last minute and then get in a panic. If you take it gently and organise your time properly you will feel a lot more calm and confident when exam time comes. Make a plan of what you want to cover each day and try to stick to it. Don't forget to include some breaks in your schedule, if you are tired it will be harder to retain the material you have been revising.

Here are a few tips for revision techniques

Go through your notes and try to summarise them

Learn the key cases, as these are essential to know

Make sure you understand how the judge has applied the law to the facts so you can do the same in an examination scenario

If the case is one you may also want to use in an essay, be sure you understand any problems it raises or solves and / or the concept of law that is involved

Example

In **Brown**, the judges decided that consent was not a defence to serious harm, so this would apply to a scenario involving GBH.

It raises a problem in the law, because the reasoning was obscure. It was not sufficiently clear why the consent defence failed. It could be argued that the defence fails if harm was intended (this would apply to **s 18** but not **s 20**), or alternatively that the defence fails if harm was serious (this would apply to both **s 18** and **s 20**).

Another problem, and one which relates to the concept of law and morals, is that some of the judges seemed to rely on their own moral values when reaching their decision.

Go through the summaries of the topic. These provide a base of the essential points which may need to be addressed

Go to the examination board's website for past exam papers, mark schemes and reports

Practice answering questions then look at the examiners' mark schemes and reports to see if you were on the right track

Revision of law and Morals

Here is a summary of the main differences between moral rules and legal rules

moral rules

- develop through opinions over time and don't change overnight
- ought to be obeyed
- are enforced by peer pressure and self-guilt
- are voluntary and apply to those who agree to be bound by them

legal rules

- can change instantly by Act of Parliament or precedent
- must be obeyed
- are enforced by the courts imposing sanctions
- are not voluntary and apply to everyone

Task 7

Taking note of the summary on the differences between legal and morals rules, give a brief description of morality.

Task 8

Briefly explain the legal rules in a way which matches the explanations of moral rules in the summary.

Task 9

Building on your answers to the previous two tasks, give an illustration (an example, case, Act or procedure) for each of the points under legal rules and develop this to include a comparison with moral rules.

There are differing views on how far the law should reflect moral values. Here's a very brief summary of the main views (dealt with in detail in 'Law and Justice').

2. Views on the relationship between law and morals

Patrick Devlin
- law and morals are related

HLA Hart
- law and morals are separate

John Stuart Mill
- the law should only interfere in moral matters where people need protection from harm

Task 10

Which judge in the **Brown** case would Professor Hart agree with and why?

Which judge would Lord Devlin agree with and why?

What do you think John Stuart Mill would have thought of the decision?

Sometimes the law changes to reflect changing moral attitudes, as with the legalisation of prostitution following the Wolfenden Committee report.

Example

Gay partnerships are an example of how laws have changed as society has changed its views. The **Civil Partnership Act 2004** allowed greater freedom for people of the same sex to enjoy many of the rights that married heterosexual couples have and in March 2014, gay marriage itself became legal when **s 1** of the **Marriage (Same Sex Couples) Act 2013** came into force.

Examination tip

Remember that morality is not just about sex, although this is a perfectly valid example; moral issues cover a wide range of subject matters. You will always gain marks for discussing other contemporary examples and cases involving a variety of moral issues. Look at the examples under the heading 'Contemporary examples of the overlap between law and morals' and make sure you can explain a few of these.

Sometimes the law has to interfere in moral matters because of a dispute between individuals.

Example

In **Quintavalle**, the courts had to decide on a moral issue because of the conflicting views of the parties to the case on the issue of 'designer' babies.

Whether in procedural law, or in the substantive areas of crime, contract or tort, the law may have a moral aspect to it. Even a positivist would recognise that there is an overlap, although they would argue that the law does not *necessarily* have a moral content.

Both morals and law are based on rules so there are bound to be similarities between them. Some laws may have no moral content but many do. Here is an example or two from the substantive law.

3. The similarities between law and morals

- many crimes are both illegal and immoral, e.g., murder and rape

- contracts are based on an exchange of promises and the law will act if these promises are broken, e.g., breach of contract leads to compensation being paid

- the law of tort can be used to protect people from harm by another's negligence, e.g., 'do not harm your neighbour' – **Donoghue**

There is also an element of morality seen in the laws against smoking in public buildings, fox hunting, drugs, and, in some areas, drinking in the street.

A general guide to examination papers

Read **all** questions carefully before deciding which to answer.

Look again at the ones you wish to answer to make sure you can do so, make brief notes – this can be a useful checklist later when you are tired and your memory begins to fail.

Structure your answer. A solid start is worth a lot and gets the examiner on your side. A small plan is helpful.

It is necessary to do more than regurgitate your notes. Never put in irrelevant material just because you know it – there is **never** a question asking you to 'write all you know about...'. You need to be selective as to what is relevant, and choose appropriate cases and examples in support of what you say.

In essay questions, you will usually be asked to form an opinion or to weigh up arguments for and against a particular statement. Here a broader range of knowledge is needed showing arguments for, arguments against and an evaluation of these arguments. You should always round off your answer with a short concluding paragraph, preferably using some of the wording from the question to indicate to the examiner that you are addressing the specific issue raised.

Essays should have a logical structure. The beginning should introduce the subject matter, the central part should explain/analyse/criticise it as appropriate, and the conclusion should bring the various strands of argument together with reference to the question set.

Try to consider alternative arguments. A well-rounded essay will bring in other views even if you disagree with them; you cannot shoot them down without setting them up first.

Here is an idea of how to structure your essay.

Writing a discussion essay: staging the information logically

If you stage your essay as follows, it will make it easy to read, logically structured and easier to write. It may also mean you don't leave out important points. Here's how it works:

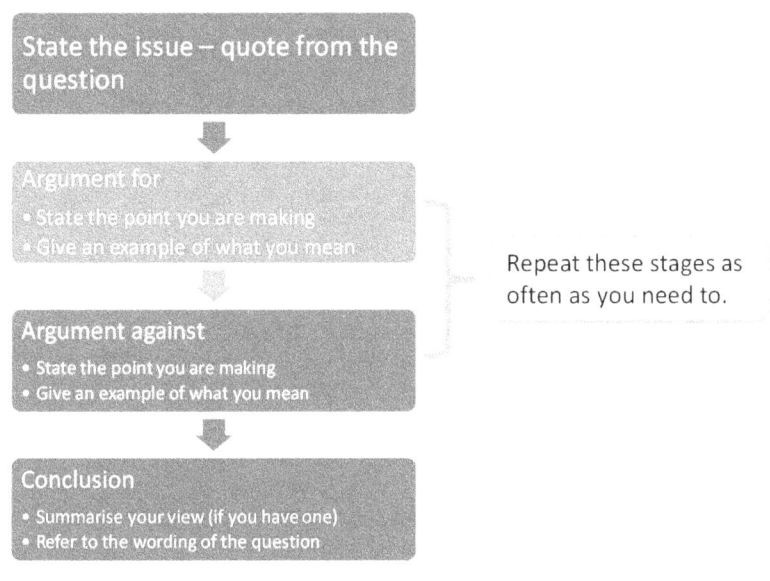

Repeat these stages as often as you need to.

Writing each paragraph: making each one logical and easy to read (and write!)

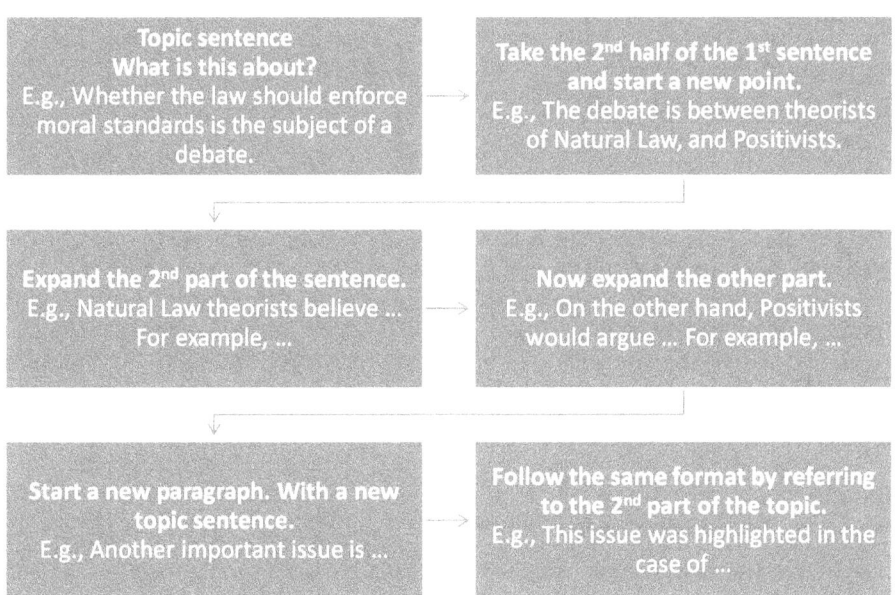

Finally, make sure you cover the whole question; there are only a certain number of marks available. The examiner has a mark scheme to work to, so however brilliant your answer to one part of the question is, missing out the other parts will severely reduce your total marks.

Examination practice for Law and Morals

Although different exam boards have different ways of styling their examination papers, there are always going to be common elements. You will need to be able to evaluate a given concept to provide a critique of the area, including case examples and reference to theorists where appropriate.

Many exam boards suggest you should use current issues and developments in the law when answering questions on jurisprudence or concepts of law. The examination question may even require recent examples, as in the question in Task 13 below. Keep an eye on current affairs and try to bring in some of your own ideas as to how far the law is, or should be, involved in issues of morality. As stated earlier, there is no right answer to these issues but if you offer your own opinion avoid being too opinionated. Remember this is a law exam, so always use the theories, cases, Acts of Parliament and / or legal procedures to support what you say.

Don't say 'I think smoking is completely wrong and the law should stop people doing it' but instead say 'I think smoking in public places is wrong and the **Health Act** is right to ban it. Although Mill argued that the law should not interfere unless harm is caused to others, smoking affects other people's quality of life, and possibly even causes physical harm through passive smoking. The **Health Act** is also a valid piece of legislation so, even though positivists like Hart do not believe the law has to have a moral content, they would say it should be obeyed'.

Task 11

Find a copy of a recent newspaper and see if you can find any references to what could be described as a moral issue. Keep a note of this as something you could refer to in an exam answer.

The 'Essay pointers' and 'Examination tips' are intended to provide you with information to use in an essay where you have to evaluate this concept of law. Look through these and your answers to the tasks before doing the evaluation practice below. There are no 'Key criticisms' in this booklet because there is no particular law to criticise; there are only different views on how law and morals connect, and how far they should do so.

One way to practise for an essay on this subject is to choose an issue that matters to you and consider how the theorists would approach it.

Example

Taking the ban on smoking as an example, Hart would say that the law was validly made by the proper procedure in Parliament so even though the law did not have to have a moral element, it was a valid law and should be obeyed. Devlin would say the law was right as it follows the moral reasoning that smoking is bad for people and so is wrong. As stated in the answer to Task 3, Mill would probably say that smoking should be a matter for individual choice, not legislation. However, he also recognised that the law might need to interfere where an activity could harm others. In the case of smoking he may say that the law needs to protect other people, e.g., from the effects of 'passive smoking'.

There is no 'right' answer to evaluation questions, opinions vary and you can form your own – but **always** use cases and/or examples to back up what you say.

The following two exercises will give you a basis for a discussion of the relationship between law and morality.

Examination practice: Task 12

Look at the following views and briefly develop the statements to say whether you agree, or not. Be sure to include an example or case to illustrate what you say.

> *Law and morals are closely connected*
>
> *Law should be separate from morals which is a matter for society alone*

The law reflects the moral views of society

The law should enforce morality on society

The law should not interfere with a person's freedoms

It is not the law's place to decide on moral issues because there is no 'shared morality'

Examination tip

You can't learn all the matters discussed in this chapter in any detail, so pick a few that make sense to you and practice writing a paragraph on these to explain the relationship between the law and the moral issue involved. There are several different contemporary examples given above so that you can pick something from these to ensure you have up-to-date examples. As you can see in the question below, this may be a necessary part of an examination answer. This task will help you prepare for such a question.

Examination practice: Task 13

Write a short essay (around 350-400 words) on the statement below, taken from an AQA examination paper. Include some reference to the theories or debates surrounding the particular area.

'Consider the extent to which the law should seek to uphold moral values and discuss why the debate concerning .law and morality continues to be important in the 21st century.'

Examination question: Task 14

The following is an example of a typical examination question

'Discuss the nature of legal and moral rules. Consider whether the law does and should reflect moral rules.'

Using the following as a guide, write out a detailed plan of what you would include in an answer to this question.

A logical approach is needed so that you keep on track of the actual question, and do not wander into irrelevant areas. It is best to divide a question like this into several parts.

A brief plan would look something like this:

> **An explanation of the nature of both legal and moral rules**
>
> **A discussion of the similarities and difference between legal and moral rules and the extent to which they overlap, with examples**
>
> **An evaluation of the extent to which the law does reflect moral values, with examples and reference to the theories and/or debates**
>
> **An evaluation of the extent to which the law should reflect moral values, with examples and reference to the theories and/or debates**

Examination tips

> You may offer your own opinion on whether the law should reflect morality; however, you must be sure that it is supported by reference to theorists, cases and/or examples

> It is not enough just to refer to a case; you need to explain how it relates to the question

The following examples refer to the 'does' and 'should' aspects of the above question

'The decision in **Brown** was influenced by morality, as was that in **R v R**. In both case moral values were taken into account in the decision, so it can be said the law **does** reflect moral values. I think that it is right that the law **should** reflect moral values so that it keeps up with changing attitudes as in **R v R**, but this may not be fair in a case like **Brown** as the conduct was in private, but they were found guilty of a criminal offence. Perhaps in this type of case the law **should not** be involved. Mill argued for the law to have a limited role in enforcing moral values, so would probably not have approved of the decision. Devlin, on the other hand, believed that the law should reflect and enforce moral values, so might have approved. Overall I think Mill is to be preferred.'

'The **Human Fertilisation and Embryo Act (HFEA)**, and the more recent changes in **HFEA 2008**, involving 'saviour siblings' or 'designer' babies, as well as the use of embryos for research and surrogacy, are examples of the law keeping up with changing technology and reflecting the majority view that such advances are not immoral. I believe that it is important that the law **does** reflect moral values in this way and that it **should** do so, otherwise morality could be frozen at a certain point in time, an argument Professor Hart used against Lord Devlin. However, the difficulties of finding a shared morality, as highlighted by Durkheim, could support an argument that the law **should not** attempt to reflect morality but instead leave it to individual choice. The fact that we do not have a 'good Samaritan' law is an example of leaving morality to individual choice. Many people would feel morally obliged to save a drowning child, currently though, it is a matter of choice and the law does not get involved unless there is a duty to act, as in **Gibbins & Proctor**. Overall, I think the law **should** sometimes reflect moral values but only where it is clear that the majority share those values.'

Task 1

The answer partly depends on your views. Murder is widely held to be immoral as well as illegal. Smoking in public is illegal but whether it is immoral is arguable. On one hand, people feel that the law should not interfere and it should be left to individual choice. On the other, many people argue that smoking can harm others, so should be illegal. Neither cheating in an examination nor swearing is illegal, but both may be viewed as immoral. Crimes such as speeding, parking on a yellow line and other traffic offences are not often seen as immoral. However, even parking on a yellow line is arguably immoral if, e.g., you are blocking an emergency exit. Adultery is immoral but legal. Lying may be immoral, and it is sometimes illegal, e.g., lying in court or in certain documents. Shoplifting is theft, and most stealing may be seen as immoral. However, this may depend on the circumstances. It may not be seen as morally wrong to steal food if someone is starving and there is no alternative.

Task 2

This will depend on your rules so this is just an illustration. You may have decided to make a rule against stealing from others, for example. You might like this to have the force of law so that it applies to everyone, and is then enforceable by your chosen method. The way of enforcing the rule could be by someone your group has elected or appointed for the purpose and to whom the group has given the power to impose punishment (sanctions) for breaking this rule. You may have another rule that bans swearing in public but decide that this can be enforced without recourse to the law. If the rule does not have the force of law then there will not be a specific punishment for breaking it. However, there may be disapproval from the rest of the group and this may have the effect of preventing most people from breaking the rule even though it is not a law.

Task 3

You could argue both these questions either way. Mill believed the law should not be involved unless harm was caused. He would probably say that the ban reduces people's freedoms and smoking should be a matter for individual choice, not legislation. However, he also recognised that the law might need to interfere where an activity could harm others. In the case of smoking he may say that the law needs to protect other people, e.g., from the effects of 'passive smoking'.

As regards the decision in **Brown**, Mill believed the law should not be involved unless harm was caused to others. As the men all consented to the harm, Mill would perhaps have allowed their appeal based on non-intervention and freedom of the individual. On the other hand, you could also argue that he may have agreed with the majority because there was sufficient harm involved for the law to intervene. Whichever you argue, it is likely his decision would be based on legal logic and not morality.

Task 4

Devlin would agree with Lord Lowry who said such activities were not *"conducive to the welfare of society"*.

Hart would agree with Lord Mustill, who took the view that although the acts were immoral that did not make them unlawful, so the conviction should be quashed.

Mill believed in freedom of the individual so would agree with Lord Slynn, who said it was not for the courts to protect people from themselves.

Task 5

As noted, there is no right answer so here is an argument for and against each.

Giving someone food against their will

For: The law should be involved if the person would die without feeding, especially if it concerns a child or a vulnerable adult

Against: Feeding should not be a matter of law but of personal choice, either for the person refusing food or the family and doctors if they are unable to make their wishes clear, or in the case of a child

Withdrawing artificial feeding from someone in a coma

For: Whether withdrawing food is in the best interests of the person concerned is best decided by a court of law after consideration of all the circumstances, as in **Re M** and **Bland**. These cases show that the court will consider the best interests of the particular patient because in Bland withdrawing food was accepted; in **Re M,** it was not.

Against: The family and doctors of the person in the coma should be able to make such decisions without the law being involved. They best know what the person concerned would have wanted and all the circumstances of the case.

Task 6

This depends on which examples you chose. Here is an example of two cases, the latter being a more contemporary issue which still causes a lot of debate today.

Airedale NHS Trust v Bland 1993

For: Even though Hart would say that law and morals are separate, this case shows that the law may have to be involved in an aspect of morality. If the court had not made a declaration that withdrawing food was permissible, the doctors could have been guilty of murder. Some people would argue that the taking of a life is never moral, perhaps reflecting Lord Devlin's views that immoral acts could weaken the fabric of society, and therefore should be punished by law. Either way the law has to be involved to regulate the behaviour of the doctors.

Against: The moral decision, in the doctor's eyes, would be to remove the tube, as there was no quality of life and he would never recover. It is better for a qualified doctor to make such decisions rather than the court. Artificial life would not be sustained if the tube were to be removed so it would not be a positive act of killing. Mill would probably argue that the law should not interfere as although the patient would die, it was in his and his family's best interests so did not harm others.

There is also an argument that the law should not have declared it legal to withdraw treatment. It is arguably immoral to withdraw feeding from a person and it would actually be less immoral to kill the patient with an injection. This would be quick and cause less anguish for the family who have to watch a slow death.

Quintavalle 2005

For: An argument for allowing couples to use tissue typing for a child in order to help another child is that it not only saves a life, but also the couple concerned should be free to choose. Mill would argue that refusing it is against the freedom of the individual, so the law should not interfere – as long as no harm is caused to others.

Against: Against this argument, one can say that it should not be allowed because if an embryo is created which does not provide a tissue match, it will be destroyed. Even if that embryo is not legally a human being, it seems immoral to destroy what is potentially a life. On the natural law theory, law should have a moral content; Devlin would argue that the law should protect society from immoral behaviour. In response to Mill's point one can argue that others are harmed by this action, because people who believe life to be sacred will feel very badly let down that the law is not upholding such moral values.

The opposing views In Brown were:

> *Lord Templeman said society is entitled to protect itself against a cult of violence and that pleasure derived from the infliction of pain was evil*

> *Lord Lowry said such activities were not conducive to the welfare of society*

> *Lord Mustill took the view that although the acts were immoral that did not make them unlawful*

> *Lord Slynn said it was not for the courts to protect people from themselves*

Hart argued that there is no widely shared morality and that law and morals are separate but Devlin took the view that law and morality are inextricably linked

*In **Quintavalle**, the HL ruled that the **Human Fertilisation and Embryology Act 1990** could be interpreted as allowing selection of embryos for selective reproduction. A further outcome was that the government issued a consultation paper to assess public opinion on these issues which resulted in the **2008 Act***

The Wolfenden Report was about homosexuality and prostitution

This is a matter of opinion, but look at the various essay pointers and tasks for some thoughts

There are several ways to answer this question. You could say something along the lines of 'morality is a code of conduct or rules which are developed gradually over time. They usually reflect the views of society as to how people should behave, and so are voluntarily accepted by members of society. There are no formal sanctions for breaking moral rules, although they can be enforced through social disapproval or peer pressure'.

Legal rules can change quickly by Act of Parliament or precedent

Legal rules must be obeyed

They are enforced by the courts

They are not voluntary and they apply to everyone

Laws can change overnight. A court case can result in a decision which changes the law in an instant, as with **R v R**. Even statute law can change relatively quickly, an example being the **Dangerous Dogs Act** which was put through Parliament hurriedly in response to public opinion. Both examples show the law responding to society's views, as has happened in relation to gay partnerships and designer babies. Moral rules develop gradually, as in the above examples. It was many years before attitudes changed and public opinion moved towards wanting changes in the law. However, once attitudes do change then the law may be influenced by this, so that once a Government is prepared to respond to public opinion, and put the matter before Parliament for debate, the law can change quickly.

Legal rules must be obeyed, so, e.g., once the smoking ban came into force people had to obey it; there was no longer an individual choice in the matter. With moral rules people ought to follow them, but there is no duty to do so. However, once a moral issue becomes a legal one then people have to obey this too; it is now no longer only a moral rule but also a legal one, as in **R v R**.

Laws are enforceable so if a legal rule is broken legal sanctions will follow. Enforcement of legal rules is done initially through the police, and then by the courts by way of sentencing and remedies. This is unlike moral rules which are not legally enforceable, although some sanctions may come from, e.g., family members. The disapproval of society in general and/or peer pressure may lead to a kind of enforcement in that people may therefore obey the rules, but they do not have to. Before smoking in public buildings became illegal, it was not socially acceptable to smoke in church or in a classroom, so people did not do because of disapproval of society, or sanctions from a priest or teacher, but there were no legal sanctions if this moral rule was disobeyed.

Legal rules apply to everyone (there are a few very minor exceptions). Using the smoking example again, it is now illegal to smoke in a public building, so nobody can do so. Before the law changed, it was purely a moral issue, so people *could* smoke in church or the classroom, but they didn't because it was seen as wrong even if not illegal. If a student smoked in class and broke this moral rule, they would be subject to the disapproval of their teachers and also probably their family, friends and society in general. However, a teacher staying in the evening to mark essays could have a cigarette without people thinking this was wrong. Unlike legal rules, moral rules are not uniform in their application.

Task 10

Professor Hart would agree with Lord Mustill because he thought the law should not interfere with the rights of the individual any more than necessary.

Lord Devlin would agree with Lord Templeman who said society was entitled to protect itself against a cult of violence and that pleasure derived from pain was evil.

John Stuart Mill would probably have thought Lord Mustill was right, because he believed the law should not interfere with the rights of the individual.

Task 11

There is no answer for this task; I hope you found something of interest though.

Examination practice: Task 12

There will be different answers here depending on your view but here is an example of how you could develop the point in each case, together with an example or a case to illustrate.

> *Law and morals are closely connected in many areas such as murder, child abuse and rape. Other laws have little moral content though, so the relationship is a mixed one. In cases of theft, there may be a morally sound reason for breaking the law, e.g., stealing milk to feed a baby so the law on theft has a relationship with morals only sometimes*

> *Law should be separate from morals because there is no 'shared morality'. People disagree regarding what is right or wrong. For this reason matters involving morals, such as abortion or adultery, and even sexual violence as in Brown, are a matter for society rather than the law*

> *The law reflects the moral views of society. This can be seen in the increasingly liberal laws on homosexuality ending with the Marriage (Same Sex Couples) Act 2013, the decision in R v R making marital rape illegal, and the ban on smoking in public*

> *The law should enforce morality on society. If people were left to choose then there would be different rules for different sections of society. Immorality, as Lord Devlin said, can lead*

to the disintegration of society, as exemplified in Brown where the law stepped in to ensure immoral behaviour does not go unpunished

I partly agree that the law should not interfere with a person's freedoms and think the decision in Brown was wrong as the people acted in private. However where someone can be hurt or discriminated against I think (as does Mill) that the law needs to step in, as in R v R which protected women from domestic violence

I agree it is not the law's place to decide on moral issues because there is no 'shared morality'. In a multi-cultural society it should be up to the various groups in society to decide on moral issues, e.g., in Begum the law ruled a girl could not argue against a school ruling on wearing a garment which covered her head to toe

There are many possible answers; what follows is just one possible approach, and you may have used different examples. The main thing is that you have addressed the points raised by the question, so not only do you need to discuss whether the law should seek to uphold moral values, but also it is vital that you use some contemporary examples to highlight why the debate concerning law and morality continues to be important in the 21st century.

As Durkheim suggested, there is no shared morality, so I don't believe the law should get involved in moral issues to any great extent. Some laws do not appear to be connected with morals, e.g., which side of the road we drive on, so these are not a problem; however, in other cases law and morals are closely connected, and if there is a dispute then may be the law is needed to act as a decision maker. The issues of euthanasia and assisted suicide illustrate that the debate about law and morals is still important today, as more cases come before the higher courts such as that of **Purdy** and, more recently, **Nicklinson 2013**. The law has to find a way to produce a result which represents a consensus but this is difficult when there are strong conflicting moral views. **Cox** and **Bland** are hard cases to reconcile; giving a lethal injection at a patient's request led to a murder charge in **Cox**, but in **Bland,** withdrawing artificial feeding was accepted as lawful. Some might say that the latter case was *more* immoral as it was a longer, drawn-out death. The law is attempting to make difficult decisions when moral issues are at stake, and although criticisms have been made euthanasia is still illegal in England. In Belgium, it has been legal for some years and in 2014, this was extended to children who are terminally ill, which caused a heated debate about the morality of such a law. Another reason the debate continues to be important in the 21st Century is advances in technology and medical knowledge. This is shown in **Quintavalle,** where the court had to make a ruling on the moral issue of whether a couple could select an embryo with certain characteristics, what is often termed 'designer babies'. Another example is downloading music on the internet and infringing copyright laws. This would be immoral to some as it takes away from the income of those who wrote or performed the songs. In conclusion, it can be said that perhaps the law has to get involved with moral issues. Changes in technology mean that new issues arise all the time, and the law also has to keep up-to-date with changing social attitudes, thus the debate continues to be of importance in the 21st century.

The first part of the question is mostly descriptive rather than evaluative, explaining the nature of the two types of rule, with examples. The second part is evaluative, analysing and evaluating the examples used in the first part with reference to the specific question as regards the 'does' and 'should' points. The theories can be brought into either part, if used in the first then you can refer back to them in the second.

You won't have time to cover everything so select those examples that makes sense to you. There may be a need to strike a balance between breadth and depth. As long as the answer is not superficial, and – most importantly – covers the specific question, a candidate who covers a greater number of theories and/or examples would be expected to do so in less detail.

The following guide gives you some ideas and refers to some of the tasks which you have covered where these would provide useful material.

Plan for the first part

Explain the characteristics of legal rules

Do the same for moral rules and compare the two (see Summary 1) - Tasks 7, 8 and 9 in the revision chapter will help with this

Add examples of where legal rules and morality coincide and where there is no moral element - See Task 1

Add a little from the theorists to show how they view the nature of legal rules (see Summary 2).

For positivists, e.g., Professor Hart, law may be based on morality, but it is not necessary that it should be. The validity of a law is not affected by whether it is morally acceptable, law and morals are separate.

For a follower of natural law, e.g., Devlin, law comes from a higher source such as God or nature. Laws must be based on moral rules and if not that law need not usually be obeyed, because it is not a true law.

Examples of where legal rules and morality coincide and where there is no moral element (see Summary 3)

Mention the problem with finding a shared morality in a multi-cultural society, with examples.

Cases on religious symbols and clothing are good examples of the problem. However, there are plenty of other instances where there is no shared morality, so use some of the examples under the different areas of law and be sure to include something from the more contemporary issues (see tasks 5 and 6).

Example

Since the Health Act 2006 came into force, smoking is illegal in a public building. This means no one can do so because the law applies to everyone and is not voluntary. When it was purely a moral issue, people could smoke in church or the classroom, because moral rules are voluntary. However, people didn't do so because they would be subject to the disapproval of family, friends and society in general. Even before smoking in public buildings became illegal, it was not socially acceptable to smoke in church or in a classroom, but was in pubs and cafés. The law has reflected morality in banning something which is harmful, but has gone further by extending the law to all public buildings.

This example could be brought into the second part instead, as part of a discussion of whether the law reflects moral values.

Plan for the second part

The second part of the question requires evaluation of the material in the first part, with emphasis on how far the law reflects moral values. Both 'does' and 'should' need addressing.

Does the law reflect moral values?

Use cases or examples to show how the law may reflect morality

The laws banning smoking in public buildings (Health Act 2006), allowing gay marriage (Marriage (Same Sex Couples) Act 2013) and making marital rape illegal (R v R) are all examples of the law changing as attitudes change, thus reflect the perceived moral values of society

Refer back to the problem with finding a shared morality in a multi-cultural society

Examples where moral values may influence the law but where the law does not necessarily reflect the moral climate, e.g., Brown

If the law reflects morality, whether it is shared or not, that law then enforces those values on society as a whole, thus the decision in Brown now applies to everyone

Reference to a range of issues, including current affairs, will enhance an answer

Examples of some contemporary issues include contraception for teenagers (Gillick), assisted suicide (Purdy), force-feeding of an anorexic (Re E), designer babies (Quintavalle) and religious clothing in schools (Begum)

Possible reference to other recent examples from the media

A brief discussion of whether the law in the examples reflected morality

Should the law reflect moral values?

This is more difficult to assess. Candidates, like academics and judges, will have different views. The main question to consider is whether the law should enforce moral issues or whether it should remain a matter for individuals or society in general to regulate their own affairs. There is no 'right answer', but you need to give some examples and mention a theorist or two. Tasks 5 and 6 will help with this, as will Task 13.

Refer back to the theories if discussed in the first part of the question, or add them now

The Wolfenden Report can be discussed as a base as it suggested changes to the law to reflect changing moral values and also that the law should not enforce certain moral values on society

Use the Hart-Devlin debate in response to the Report to illustrate that there is no consensus. Therefore, it is arguable that the law should not reflect moral rules where there is no agreement on those rules

You could then bring this more up to date by reference to the Civil Partnership Act 2004 and the Marriage (Same Sex Couples) Act 2013

Several cases or examples are needed, but you can refer to ones used above e.g., moral values may influence the law, as in R v R, Brown, which then enforces those values on society as a whole

Refer back to the problem that there is unlikely to be a shared morality in a multi-cultural society, e.g., Quintavalle, Begum

This can include reference to the question of whose values the law is reflecting, e.g., in Brown, the law reflected the judges' views but it is debatable whether these were widely shared within society as a whole

Use of current affairs or reference back to earlier examples, e.g., the problems of advancing technology making moral decisions necessary as in the 'saviour siblings' and the Siamese twins cases (Quintavalle and Re A). These and cases such as Purdy and Nicklinson on assisted suicide show the debate on law and morals is a continuing one

In a full answer, you will need to develop some of your examples – see next paragraph and the final 'Examination tips' and examples in the Revision chapter

Medical and technological advances mean procedures become possible which many think are immoral but which others see as providing a better quality of life. This shows the problem with finding a 'shared morality' to reflect. In Quintavalle, the law did not reflect the morality of the group who argued the case, but decided the Act could be used to allow people to choose, a view Mill would approve of

Another possible view is that the law should enforce morality to a greater extent than it does, e.g., there is no 'good Samaritan' law in England. This can be supported by case examples where no duty was found (Khan) with alternative cases such as Gibbins & Proctor or Pittwood to illustrate why we may not need such a law because the courts can reflect morality by finding a duty in certain situations

It is important in an examination to finish with a strong concluding paragraph. This should briefly sum up your arguments referring to the wording of the question, e.g., to the words 'does' and 'should', to show you have addressed the specific points raised.

Example

"It can be seen from the above examples that there are times when the law does reflect morality; however the extent to which it should is more debateable. Where it is the judges' own opinion of right and wrong, rather than that of society, I think the law should not interfere. It is hard to reconcile the cases of **Brown** and **Wilson** and these show why judges should not attempt to reflect moral values. When Parliament reflects moral values as in the **Health Act 2006** and the **Marriage (Same Sex Couples) Act 2013**, it is more acceptable because Parliament has been elected by members of society. Overall I believe that in a multi-cultural society such as exists today the law should only interfere when harm can be caused to others, as Mill suggested."

The following abbreviations are commonly used. You may use them in an examination answer, but write them in full the first time, e.g., write 'actual bodily harm (ABH)' and then after that you can just write 'ABH'.

General

Draft Code – A Criminal Code for England and Wales (Law Commission No. 177), 1989

CCRC Criminal Cases Review Commission

ABH actual bodily harm

GBH grievous bodily harm

D defendant

C claimant

V Victim

CA Court of Appeal

HL House of Lords

SC Supreme Court

Acts

S – section (thus **s 1** Theft Act 1968 refers to section 1 of that Act)

s 1(2) means section 1 subsection 2 of an Act.

OAPA – Offences against the Person Act 1861

In cases – these don't need to be written in full

CC (at beginning) chief constable

CC (at end) county council

BC borough council

DC district council

LBC London borough council

AHA Area Health Authority

J Justice

LJ Lord Justice

LCJ Lord Chief Justice

LC Lord Chancellor

AG Attorney General

CPS Crown Prosecution Service

DPP Director of Public Prosecutions

AG Attorney General

Acknowledgements

I am grateful to the following for examination questions.

The Assessment and Qualification Alliance (AQA)

Note: Where worked solutions to, and / or commentaries on, AQA questions or possible answers are provided it is the author who is responsible for them. They have not been provided or approved by AQA and do not necessarily constitute the only possible solutions.

I am also grateful to my husband, Dave, for many hours of proof reading and for his hard work on the diagrams.

www.ingramcontent.com/pod-product-compliance
Lightning Source LLC
Chambersburg PA
CBHW070728180526
45167CB00004B/1672